For Orlando and Eleanor—M.B.

For Nick and Dylan, my sunflowers!—E.B.

Published in association with the Van Gogh Museum.

Dear Vincent © 2024 Thames & Hudson Ltd, London
Text © 2024 Michael Bird
Illustrations © 2024 Ella Beech

First published in 2024 in the United States of America by
Thames & Hudson Inc., 500 Fifth Avenue, New York, New York 10110

Libary of Congress Control Number 2024933370

ISBN   978-0-500-65338-8

Printed and bound in China by Toppan Leefung Printing Limited

Be the first to know about our new releases,
exclusive content and author events by visiting
thamesandhudson.com
thamesandhudsonusa.com
thamesandhudson.com.au

Dear Vincent

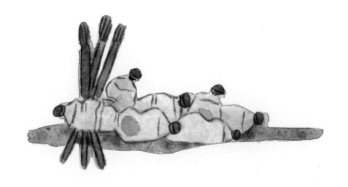

Michael Bird

Illustrated by Ella Beech

Vincent is an artist. He is always drawing and painting.

"I wish my paintings were better," thinks Vincent, "but one day I will paint the picture of my dreams."

Theo is Vincent's brother and his best friend.
He likes to be helpful to Vincent,
and often writes to him.

Dear Vincent,
I hope you are well,
I hope you are happy.
Is there anything you need?

Vincent is not well.
Vincent is not happy.
He has a stomach ache.

It is winter and the gray city is wet and cold.
The other artists do not understand him.
Nobody wants to buy his paintings.

"I need to go away," thinks Vincent.

"I need sunshine, and fresh air,
and good food, and new friends."

When Vincent gets home,
he finds a message from Theo.

Dear Vincent,
Here is a
train
ticket to
the Sunny South.

·ARLES·

He is so excited! He starts
packing his bag right away.

He puts in eleven paintbrushes,

four big drawing books,

a bottle of turpentine,

a tin of poppyseed oil,

and twenty-one different colors of paint.

He puts in his toothbrush, pajamas, and socks. But the bag will not stay shut.

"I know," says Vincent. "I can leave out my toothbrush and socks!"

Vincent hurries to the railroad station.

"All aboard!"

The conductor blows his whistle and off they go.

"Goodbye, gray city!" shouts Vincent.

They race through the countryside.
What can Vincent see?

Fields, clouds, trees,
a horse and cart trundling along,
and children waving as the train thunders past.

Vincent waves back. "Hello!" he calls,
"I'm on my way to the Sunny South!"

The train arrives in a little town.
Vincent leaps down onto the platform.

But where has the sun gone?
Where are the bright,
warm colors?

Oh no!

It is snowing.

GROCERY

Vincent's fingertips feel like icicles.
His nose feels like a frozen raspberry.

"Look at that scruffy artist,"
say the people.

Luckily, it is not long before the sun comes out
and the snow melts away.

In an orchard outside the town
Vincent sees apple and peach trees
covered in white and pink blossom.

He opens his bag and takes out
his paints and brushes.

He paints a picture of the flowering trees,
and the fresh green grass, and the calm blue sky.

"I will send this picture to Theo," he decides.

Theo hangs Vincent's picture in his study.

"It's just like looking through a
window on a sunny day," he thinks.

Dear Vincent,
 Thank you for the wonderful painting.
 I am going to send you lots more paints
 so you can paint as many pictures
 as you want.

Today Vincent goes exploring. He walks past a farm
where a farmer is planting seeds.

"Good morning!" says Vincent.
"What sort of seeds are those?"

"Sunflower seeds," says the farmer.
"Here. Take a look."

The sunflower seeds are small, and hard, and stripy.

"How can sunflowers come out of those tiny seeds?" thinks Vincent.

He pushes a seed into the soil.

When Vincent gets back to the little town,
Postman Joseph is waiting with an enormous package.

"Is it your birthday?" he asks.

Vincent tears open the package.

"It's from Theo!"

The package is full of tubes of paint. On the labels are the names of all the different colors.

"I must paint a new picture right away," exclaims Vincent. "Can I paint your portrait?"

PRUSSIAN BLUE

CHROME ORANGE

RAW SIENNA

ZINC WHITE

VERMILION

"I have never had my portrait painted before,"
says Postman Joseph.

"You must sit in this chair and stay very still,"
Vincent explains.

"You must not

w^ave your arms, or

jiggle your legs, or

wiggle your beard."

"Can I sneeze?" asks Postman Joseph.

"All right," Vincent agrees.
"But only because we are friends."

"Achoooo!"

Postman Joseph brings all his family
to meet Vincent. "Please paint
our portraits too!" they say.

Here is his wife, Madame Augustine,
and schoolboy Camille, and baby Marcelle,
and Armand, who looks very grown-up
with his little moustache and his big blue hat.

"You must promise to sit still,"
Postman Joseph tells them.
"And no yawning or sneezing!"

Vincent has painted so many new pictures.
He has made new friends.

But he still wants to be
a better painter.

"One day soon," he tells
himself, "I will paint the
picture of my dreams!"

He hangs his pictures around his bedroom, so that he can look at them while he is sitting in bed, or eating his breakfast, or cleaning his brushes.

The springtime is turning into summer.

"What has happened to my sunflower seed?"
Vincent wonders.

On a hot day, he puts on a straw hat
and goes out into the fields.

There it is!

Where he planted the seed,
a leafy stalk is growing.
It is almost as tall as Vincent.

The sunflower leaves are emerald green.
The sky is ultramarine.

But one color is missing.

Vincent goes to a café to meet his friends
and read his letters from Theo.

Dear Vincent,
How are you getting on in the Sunny South?
Do you need any new clothes or paints?

It is the hottest day of summer. Vincent walks along
the road that leads out of the town. The fields shimmer
in the heat. A grasshopper springs across his path.

And here is his sunflower. It has grown so tall!

Vincent looks up into its wide,
round face, ringed by petals
like gleaming yellow flames.

The next morning, Vincent arranges a big bunch of sunflowers in a vase.

Then he takes the new tubes of paint that Theo has sent and squeezes out the colors, one by one.

The yellow paints gleam like flowers.

The flowers glow like the sun.

"This is it!" shouts Vincent,
"This is the picture of my dreams!"

Outside in the fields the sun beats down
and the sunflowers shine

yellow,

yellow,

yellow,

as far as the eye can see.

Theo is very proud of all the paintings that Vincent
has sent to him. He invites some visitors to look at them.

A lady and gentleman arrive with their little girl.
"What do you think of my brother's pictures?" he asks.

"That postman's uniform is too blue," complains the gentleman.

"The flowers are too yellow," says the lady.

"The colors are much too colorful," they agree.

"We are going now. Goodbye."

The little girl does not want to leave.
"Come along, Marie!" say her parents.
But she keeps looking at the pictures.

She likes Postman Joseph's
blue uniform.

"Hurry up, slowpoke!"
calls her mother.

The pink blossoms make her feel
as if she is playing in a lovely garden
in the spring sunshine.

"You'll make us late!"
grumbles her father.

The golden sunflowers
give her a happy feeling.

Before she goes, Marie turns round for

one

last

look.

"Goodbye,"
she whispers in her
smallest, secret voice.

"Thank you, dear Vincent."